AF270462

WASHINGTON
NATIONALS

BY ANTHONY K. HEWSON

SportsZone

An Imprint of Abdo Publishing
abdobooks.com

abdobooks.com

Published by Abdo Publishing, a division of ABDO, PO Box 398166, Minneapolis, Minnesota 55439. Copyright © 2023 by Abdo Consulting Group, Inc. International copyrights reserved in all countries. No part of this book may be reproduced in any form without written permission from the publisher. SportsZone™ is a trademark and logo of Abdo Publishing.

Printed in the United States of America, North Mankato, Minnesota.
102022
012023

Cover Photo: G. Fiume/Getty Images Sport/Getty Images
Interior Photos: David J. Phillip/AP Images, 4; John Lent/AP Images, 7; Sporting News/Getty Images, 8; Focus on Sport/Getty Images, 10, 13; David Durochik/AP Images, 14; Focus on Sport/Getty Images Sport/Getty Images, 17; Ronald C. Modra/Getty Images Sport/Getty Images, 20; Brian Bahr/Allsport/Getty Images Sport/Getty Images, 23; Doug Benc/Getty Images Sport/Getty Images, 25; Eliot J. Schechter/Getty Images Sport/Getty Images, 27; Billie Weiss/Boston Red Sox/Getty Images Sport/Getty Images, 28; G. Fiume/Getty Images Sport/Getty Images, 30; Rob Carr/Getty Images Sport/Getty Images, 33; Scott Cunningham/Getty Images Sport/Getty Images, 34; Tim Warner/Getty Images Sport/Getty Images, 39; Brandon Sloter/Icon Sportswire/AP Images, 40

Editor: Steph Giedd
Series Designer: Becky Daum

Library of Congress Control Number: 2022940479

Publisher's Cataloging-in-Publication Data

Names: Hewson, Anthony K., author.
Title: Washington Nationals / by Anthony K. Hewson
Description: Minneapolis, Minnesota: Abdo Publishing, 2023 | Series: Inside MLB | Includes online
resources and index.
Identifiers: ISBN 9781098290375 (lib. bdg.) | ISBN 9781098275570 (ebook)
Subjects: LCSH: Washington Nationals (Baseball team)--Juvenile literature. | Baseball teams--Juvenile
literature. | Professional sports--Juvenile literature. | Sports franchises--Juvenile literature. | Major
League Baseball (Organization)--Juvenile literature.
Classification: DDC 796.35764--dc23

TABLE OF CONTENTS

HERE COME THE EXPOS

Howie Kendrick strode to the plate in Game 7 of the 2019 World Series. With one man on base in the seventh inning, his Washington Nationals needed a big hit. They trailed the Houston Astros 2–1.

Kendrick was not a superstar. But he had played like one throughout the playoffs for the Nats. He was a big reason why they were there in their first World Series.

Kendrick swung wildly at the first pitch. On the next pitch, he got a cut fastball low and away. Kendrick reached out and took the pitch the other way, deep down the right-field line. Astros right fielder George Springer raced to try to catch it.

Howie Kendrick makes contact with his go-ahead home run in Game 7 of the 2019 World Series.

He had no chance. The ball kept soaring until it clanged off the foul pole for an amazing home run.

Kendrick pumped both fists and yelled as he ran the bases. His team was now just a few innings away from winning its first World Series. The Nats just had to hang on.

MAKING IT IN MONTREAL

Nationals fans didn't have to wait long to see their team play for a championship. The team played its first game in Washington in 2005. But the history of the team goes back way further than that.

The Canadian city of Montreal, Quebec, had been home to pro baseball since the 1890s. The minor league Montreal Royals played in the city from 1897 to 1960. They became the minor league team for the Brooklyn Dodgers of Major League Baseball (MLB) in 1939.

Around the same time, Montreal started to be considered a big-league city. In 1933 the St. Louis Browns were looking to move to a new city. Montreal was seen as a possible destination. But the Browns later moved to Baltimore and became the Orioles.

Montreal remained a minor league city, but fans loved their Royals. One of the most famous Royals was Jackie Robinson, who played in Montreal in 1946. Robinson broke the "color line"

Jackie Robinson crosses home plate after hitting a home run for the Montreal Royals in 1946.

the following year with the Dodgers as the first Black player to play in the modern major leagues. After the Royals moved in 1960, there were more efforts to make Montreal a big-league city.

Montreal's next best chance at an MLB team came later in the 1960s. MLB planned to add four new teams for 1969. Montreal was a contender but lacked a new stadium.

Montreal played at Jarry Park from 1969 to 1976.

However, Montreal's long minor league history was a positive. And the city had just hosted a World's Fair, Expo 67. There was also an ownership group in place ready to pay the $10 million expansion fee.

On May 28, 1968, Montreal and San Diego were both awarded National League (NL) expansion teams. But there were problems for Montreal. Some of the team's owners started backing out. Plans to secure a temporary stadium fell through. The future of a Montreal team was in doubt.

NL president Warren Giles came to visit Montreal. He toured a tiny stadium called Jarry Park where fans were enjoying a baseball game. If the stadium could be expanded from 3,000 to 30,000, it could work, he said. New grandstands had to be built down the left- and right-field lines and in the outfield.

The team also settled its ownership issues. Charles Bronfman became the majority owner, and John McHale was the team president. By August, just eight months before Opening Day, baseball in Montreal was back on.

THE FIRST SEASON

All the new team needed was a name. Reusing *Royals* was one popular option. But the American League (AL) team starting in 1969 in Kansas City had already taken it. Instead, *Expos* won as the name, as Montreal had just hosted Expo 67.

Montreal's big-league dreams came to life on April 8, 1969. The Expos opened their first season in New York against the Mets. Jim "Mudcat" Grant started on the mound for Montreal.

Rusty Staub joined the Expos for their opening season in 1969 and led the team in home runs.

He had been an All-Star just a few years earlier. Grant was one of the few true stars on the team.

However, Grant didn't make it out of the second inning. The game was a shootout. It was another Montreal All-Star, Rusty Staub, who made the biggest impact. Staub was 2-for-3 with a homer in the Expos' 11–10 victory.

After snow had been cleared from the field, more than 29,000 fans packed into chilly Jarry Park six days later for the first MLB game in Canada. Facing the St. Louis Cardinals, the Expos' Mack Jones clubbed a three-run homer in the first. The Expos lost a 6–0 lead but hung on to win 8–7.

The thrills kept coming early on for the new team and its fans. On April 17, the Expos faced the Phillies in Philadelphia.

Journeyman pitcher Bill Stoneman started for Montreal. Stoneman was looking for his first win of the season. He got that and more, tossing the first no-hitter in Expos history.

But there were few other highlights in the Expos' first season. They went on to lose 110 games. That tied them with fellow newcomer San Diego for the worst record in baseball that season.

BUILDING SOMETHING

The Expos eventually improved, but they did not post a winning record for their first 10 years. Despite all the losses, fans embraced their team and its stars. The biggest one was Staub, known in French-speaking Montreal as *le Grand Orange*, or "the Big Orange." The red-haired power hitter was beloved by Expos fans on and off the field. He made an effort to learn French, and he lived in Montreal all year round.

Then there was Stoneman, who would throw another no-hitter in 1972. Fans also loved pitcher Claude Raymond, a native of Montreal. But even with these fan favorites, all the losses eventually kept fans away from the ballpark. By 1976 the Expos were drawing only a little over half the fans they had been in 1969.

One reason was Jarry Park. The stadium was never meant to be the Expos' permanent home. They were supposed to have

THE BIG OWE

had a new stadium by 1972. But that venue, Olympic Stadium, did not open until 1976. The Expos began playing there in 1977.

After the move, attendance more than doubled. The new stadium attracted fans, but soon, so did the team. The Expos had built a talented core of players that included outfielders Tim Raines and Andre Dawson and superstar catcher Gary Carter. Montreal posted its first winning record in 1979 and finished second in the NL East division.

After finishing second again in 1980, the Expos were in the hunt in 1981. But a players' strike interrupted the season in June with the Expos in third place, four games behind the Philadelphia Phillies. As a result, the season was split in half. The Expos would get another chance when the season resumed on August 10. If the Expos could post the best record in the second part of the season, they'd play the Phillies, the winner of the first half of the season, in a playoff series.

The Expos struggled at first. At one point they were 14–15. Steadily they improved. But then they got hot. They went 16–8 down the stretch to win the second half of the season with a

Expos outfielder and 1977 Rookie of the Year Andre Dawson, *right*, celebrates with his teammate after hitting a home run.

30-23 record. For the first time, there would be playoff baseball in Montreal.

THE GLORY YEARS

When the Expos of the 1970s or '80s needed to win a game, fans hoped to have Steve Rogers on the mound. Rogers played his entire 13-year career with Montreal. He made five All-Star teams and was routinely among the best pitchers in baseball. But he was most remembered for what he did in the 1981 playoffs, including one legendary mistake.

The Expos played the Philadelphia Phillies in the first NL Divisional Series (NLDS) in 1981. And the matchup was a tough one. The Phillies were the defending World Series champions.

Rogers outdueled future Hall of Famer Steve Carlton to win Game 1 at Olympic Stadium. Gary Carter mashed a two-run

Five-time All-Star Steve Rogers winds up to pitch for the Expos.

home run in Game 2 to put the Expos up 2–0 in the series. However, the Phillies found some magic when the series shifted to Philadelphia. The Phillies won two straight to set up a winner-take-all Game 5.

It was a rematch of Rogers and Carlton. Rogers was shaky to start but soon settled in. He would end up pitching one of the best games of his career. Rogers shut out the Phillies in nine innings. He also knocked a two-run single to center field in the fifth inning. Those were all the runs the Expos needed as they won 3–0 to win their first playoff series.

BLUE MONDAY

Things didn't get any easier for the Expos in the NL Championship Series (NLCS). The Los Angeles Dodgers were loaded with stars. They had a team of six All-Stars and the best pitcher in the NL, Cy Young Award winner Fernando Valenzuela.

After starting Game 5 in the NLDS, Rogers wasn't rested enough to start until Game 3 of the NLCS. The series was tied at 1–1 when it shifted back to Olympic Stadium. Rogers again pitched nine strong innings, allowing just a single run. Jerry White hit a three-run homer to give the Expos a 4–1 win. The Dodgers then won Game 4 to force another deciding Game 5.

On a cold, rainy day at Olympic Stadium, Valenzuela allowed one run in the first inning but then kept the Expos' bats quiet.

Expos catcher Gary Carter played 12 of his 19 MLB season with Montreal.

The Dodgers tied the game in the fifth, and both teams struggled to push across the winning run. To keep the game tied in the ninth, Expos manager Jim Fanning turned to Rogers. He wasn't rested enough to start, but Fanning hoped his team's best arm had enough life to finish off the game.

Rogers had made just two relief appearances in his career. But he was easily the team's best pitcher overall. He got the first two outs no problem. Then Dodgers veteran Rick Monday came to the plate and hammered a 3–1 pitch over the fence in center field. The Expos got two runners on in the bottom of the ninth but couldn't score. Their magical run was over.

To Expos fans, October 19 became known as "Blue Monday." But fans were ready to move on quickly. Their team was still loaded with talent, and many expected Montreal to still be a contender the following year.

HUNGRY FOR MORE

The Expos had one of the most exciting rosters in baseball in the 1980s. Dawson was a speedy outfielder who could hit. Raines was one of the best base stealers in the game. Carter was one of the best-hitting catchers ever.

Montreal had only two losing seasons in the 1980s. But even its winning seasons weren't enough to make the playoffs again. By 1990 the core of the 1981 team was all gone.

A new core of players developed by the early 1990s. There was Canadian slugger Larry Walker. There was do-it-all outfielder Moisés Alou and his father, Felipe, the team's manager. And there was ace Dennis Martinez, who would throw the first Expos perfect game in 1991.

Soon the Expos were winning again, finishing second in the NL East in 1992 and 1993. Although Martinez left after the 1993

HISTORY IN MONTREAL

MLB all-time hits leader Pete Rose spent just 95 games of his career in Montreal. Rose signed with the Expos before the 1984 season. He had one of the lowest batting averages of his career, but he gave fans one memorable moment. On April 13, 1984, Rose became just the second player in MLB history to reach 4,000 career hits.

season, Montreal acquired another ace named Martinez. Pedro Martinez anchored the Expos' rotation for years to come.

WHAT COULD HAVE BEEN

By 1994 the Expos had one of the best teams in baseball. As the summer heated up, they surged into first place and went 37–16 in June and July.

While the Expos were having their best season yet, rumors swirled of another players' strike. On August 11, the Expos had the best record in MLB at 74–40. The next day, players went on strike, and the season was brought to a halt.

Fans and players hoped the season would just be delayed. But the players and owners weren't making much progress on resolving their disputes. Finally, on September 14, MLB commissioner Bud Selig canceled the rest of the season. The Expos' great season was wiped away just like that.

Fans could only wonder what that Expos team would have been able to do. The team had five All-Stars. Leading up to the strike, they were on a run of 20–3. But nobody got the chance to find out.

FROM QUEBEC TO THE CAPITAL

The 1994 players' strike dragged on into 1995. When it was time to play baseball again, some of Montreal's star players were due new contracts. For years the Expos had some of the lowest player salaries in baseball. Team president Claude Brochu chose not to keep players that he knew the team could not afford to pay.

For the Expos, this meant almost all the key players from the 1994 team. Some players were simply not retained. Larry Walker was not offered a new deal, and he signed with the Colorado Rockies. Other players were traded for minor league players who were far away from making an impact in the big

Montreal left fielder Tim Raines poses in Olympic Stadium in 1984. It was home to the Expos from 1977 to 2004.

leagues. Giving away so many great players led fans to call it "the fire sale."

The Expos' financial problems affected more than their roster. The team felt the aging Olympic Stadium was not suitable for an MLB team. A new stadium, owners said, would help them make more money and afford star players.

But the owners said they did not have the money to build a stadium themselves. And the Quebec government had no interest in funding one. So the Expos played on at Olympic Stadium as attendance began to dwindle.

Not all players left in the fire sale right away. Pedro Martinez developed into one of the best pitchers in baseball. In 1997 he won the first Cy Young Award in Expos history. But a week later, he was traded too.

In 1998 a young free swinger named Vladimir Guerrero played his first full MLB season and crushed 38 home runs. Guerrero would become an annual All-Star and Most Valuable Player (MVP) candidate, one of the bright spots of the last days of the Expos.

THE END

By the time Guerrero was mashing homers at Olympic Stadium, few fans were left to see them. In 2001 Expos attendance was just under 643,000. That was the lowest in team history.

Outfielder Vladimir Guerrero established himself as one of baseball's great power hitters during his eight seasons with the Expos from 1996 to 2003.

Without a new stadium, it seemed more likely the Expos would move. Or maybe they would be eliminated entirely. An MLB plan in 2001 to eliminate two teams included the Expos and Minnesota Twins. Only a lawsuit that prevented the Twins from breaking their stadium lease saved both clubs.

That still did not resolve the Expos' situation. With the team in such a financial mess, MLB took over ownership in 2001.

The league would figure out what to do with the Expos once and for all.

On the field, the Expos were surprisingly in the playoff hunt in 2002. They even traded for some pitching help in Bartolo Colón a month before the deadline. However, the team soon faded out of the race.

Until the Expos had a permanent home, MLB decided on a temporary one. Starting with the 2003 season, the Expos played part of their schedule in San Juan, Puerto Rico. The US territory was full of baseball fans. There was one problem though. They weren't necessarily Expos fans. As a result, the team didn't have much of a home-field advantage playing in Puerto Rico.

THE LAST EXPO

Another playoff run faded in 2003. In 2004 Guerrero was traded, and the Expos collapsed to a record of 67–95. On the morning of their final home game, the news became official. The Expos were moving. They were off to Washington, DC.

That night, the Expos played in front of an enthusiastic crowd of more than 30,000 fans.

"The Last Expo" Brad Wilkerson, *right*, congratulates his teammate Vladimir Guerrero, *left*, after he scores in a 2003 game.

Some fans cried, and some cheered thanks. The scoreboard read thank you in both English and French.

CAPITAL BASEBALL

The US capital had been talked about as a home for a baseball team for some time. After all, Washington, DC, had housed many major league teams in the past. The first Washington Nationals played in the short-lived Union Association in 1884.

The city also had four major league teams named the Washington Senators. The first played in the NL from 1886 to 1989. Another formed in 1891 and lasted nine seasons. The longest-lasting version played in the AL from 1901 to 1960. A year later, they moved to Minnesota and became the Twins. They were quickly replaced by a new Washington Senators team in time for the 1961 season. But after struggling for 11 years, that franchise became the Texas Rangers.

By 2005 Washington, DC, had been without professional baseball for more than three decades. But baseball fans dreamed of having a team again. When the Expos were in the market for a new home, Washington beat out other cities such as Las Vegas, Nevada, and Portland, Oregon.

RETIRED NUMBERS

The Expos honored four legendary players by retiring their uniform numbers from future use: Andre Dawson (10), Gary Carter (8), Rusty Staub (10), and Tim Raines (30). The Nationals did not carry over these retirements. Instead, these players were honored with a banner at the home of the Montreal Canadiens hockey team.

WHAT'S OLD IS NEW

The Expos moved right into the Senators' old home of RFK Stadium. The city planned to build the team a new home within a few years. Some people also wanted the new team to take the Senators name. Some suggested calling the team the Grays as a tribute to a former

Montreal pitcher Liván Hernández winds up in his first season with the Expos in 2004.

Negro Leagues team called the Homestead Grays that played in the area.

Washington's old AL team was named the Nationals, but the name never caught on with fans. So the new owners hoped it could have another chance with Washington's new team. The Nationals also adopted a patriotic red, white, and blue color scheme. And they revived an old Senators curly *W* logo for their caps.

The Nationals kept Expos manager Frank Robinson and several players, including pitcher Liván Hernández. Hernández started the first game in Nationals history on April 4, 2005. Hernández took the loss, but he then got a win in the team's

Ryan Zimmerman waves to the home crowd in his final game at Nationals Park in 2021.

home opener 10 days later. The Nationals were even in first place at that early stage. They went on to finish 81–81.

THE PLAN

In a way, the Nationals did not seem all that different from the Expos in terms of player salaries. For their first few seasons in Washington, the Nats didn't spend big on players either. But that was part of a strategy to build a long-term winner.

The Nationals wanted to draft and develop young players. Then when those players developed into stars, they would surround them with talented free agents. One of those young players was Ryan Zimmerman. He was the Nationals' first-ever draft pick in 2005. He flew through the minors to make his MLB debut that same year. By 2009 he was an All-Star. Zimmerman went on to play his entire 16-year career in Washington.

Not every young player turned out to be a star like Zimmerman. The short-term impact of the Nationals' plan meant a lot of losses. In 2008 and 2009, the Nationals managed just 59 wins each season. That was the worst in team history since the 1976 Expos.

But those losing years meant high draft picks. In the 2009 draft, the Nationals used the first overall pick on pitcher Stephen Strasburg. The following year, they used the first overall pick on outfielder Bryce Harper. Those players helped shape the team in the decade to come.

A 50-YEAR WAIT

In 2008 the Nationals truly began to feel at home in Washington. Their new stadium, Nationals Park, opened that season. President George W. Bush was there to throw out the first pitch. And Ryan Zimmerman blasted a walk-off home run, solidifying the win for the home team.

Slowly the Nationals built themselves into winners. Stephen Strasburg made his major league debut in 2010. Fans had been eagerly awaiting his arrival. He had excelled in college at San Diego State University. He also starred for Team USA at the 2008 Olympics. When he arrived in the majors, fans couldn't wait to see what he could do.

Stephen Strasburg made his major league debut with the Nationals on June 8, 2010, at Nationals Park.

Bryce Harper followed in 2012. Harper, too, was a hugely exciting player. Baseball scouts had talked about him since he was 12. He only got better from there. Harper was known as a five-tool player. These players had a rare blend of hitting for average and power. They were also known for their good speed, strong throwing arms, and solid fielding.

These two young stars were the focus of the Nationals' playoff hopes. In between their debuts, the team signed top free agent Jayson Werth in 2011. The Nationals were entering the phase of their plan in which they aimed to be a playoff team.

The 19-year-old Harper provided a big boost to the 2012 Nationals. He hit 22 home runs, made the All-Star Team, and was named Rookie of the Year. He also played great in the outfield with a flashy style that fans loved. And the Nats needed him, as injuries limited Werth to 81 games.

That season the Nationals won 98 games, the most in team history. They won the NL East for the first time ever in a full season. And Werth provided one of the team's most memorable moments since moving to Washington.

In the NLDS against the St. Louis Cardinals, the Nationals were facing elimination in Game 4. In a tie game in the bottom of the ninth, Werth worked a 13-pitch at bat. On the 13th pitch, a fastball, he hit a walk-off homer into the visitor's

Jayson Werth celebrates upon reaching home plate after hitting his walk-off solo home run against the St. Louis Cardinals in Game 4 of the NLDS.

bullpen in left field. But heartbreak followed the next day as Washington blew a 6–0 lead in Game 5 to lose the series.

PLAYOFF DISAPPOINTMENTS

The 2012 to 2019 seasons were the best in the history of the franchise. The team had a winning record each year, won four division titles, and made the playoffs five times. The plan was paying off.

Six-time All-Star Bryce Harper blasts a grand slam against the Atlanta Braves in 2017.

The core of the Nationals team was assembled through the draft. All-Stars Harper, Anthony Rendon, Strasburg, and Zimmerman were all Nationals draft picks. The team also did well with trades and free agent signings. The Nats got star shortstop Trea Turner in a 2014 trade.

Ace pitcher Max Scherzer was signed to the biggest contract in team history in 2015. Scherzer came to Washington having recently won the AL Cy Young Award in 2013. The fiery, intense righty was one of the best strikeout pitchers in baseball.

It was no wonder the Nationals were contenders every year. But the Nats' playoff runs usually ended with heartbreaking losses. Washington lost the NLDS in five games three times. In 2018 the Nats finished 82–80. They missed the playoffs for the first time in three seasons. And worst of all, Harper left after the season to sign with the Philadelphia Phillies.

A NEW NATTITUDE

Heading into the 2019 season, the emergence of Juan Soto helped make up for the loss of Harper. Soto had been runner-up for Rookie of the Year in 2018. And the team had a healthy Howie Kendrick again. The second baseman had been limited by injury to 40 games in 2018.

But in the early part of the season, the Nationals appeared to miss their superstar outfielder. They were 12–16 at the end of April. By May 23, they'd fallen to 19–31. They were 10 games back in the NL East.

There were a lot of reasons for the Nationals' struggles. Rendon, Soto, and Turner had all dealt with injuries. And the

normally reliable bullpen had given up some leads.
Slowly those trends began to turn around. Washington
bounced back to go 18–8 in June. The Nationals were too far
back to make a run at the division title but were in the thick of
the wild-card race.

On September 24, the Nationals won the second game of a
doubleheader against Harper and the Phillies. After the game,
players and fans stayed to watch the end of the Cubs vs. Pirates
game on the Nationals Park video board. When the Cubs lost,
a celebration began. That loss clinched a playoff spot for the
Nationals. They had gone 74–38 since their 19–31 start.

REACHING NEW HEIGHTS

Because the Nats hadn't won the division, they had to play a
one-game playoff just to make the NLDS. At home in Nationals
Park, Scherzer allowed three runs in five innings. But Soto
drove in two runs, and an error brought in a third in the eighth
inning to rescue the Nats and keep their run going.

Facing the Los Angeles Dodgers in the NLDS, the Nationals
lost Games 1 and 3 but won Games 2 and 4. The Game 4
win set up a winner-take-all Game 5 at Dodger Stadium. The
game went into extra innings. Kendrick had his first chance at
being the hero. In the top of the 10th, with the bases loaded,

he blasted a grand slam deep to center field. The Nationals franchise had won a playoff series for the first time since 1981.

The Nationals stormed through the St. Louis Cardinals in the NLCS. After already being named the MVP of the NLDS, Kendrick was MVP of the NLCS, too. He hit .333 with four runs batted in. Washington swept away St. Louis to make its first World Series.

Washington had a dream start to the Fall Classic. Scherzer and Strasburg were sharp, and the offense did damage as the Nats won the first two games of the series against the Houston Astros. The series then shifted back to Washington, but the home team could not find much advantage. Houston won all three games to put the Nationals on the brink of elimination.

Strasburg took the mound in Game 6 and turned in 8 1/3 innings, allowing just two runs. Rendon drove in five runs as the Nationals won 7–2. That set up a Game 7.

In another pitchers' duel, the Astros had a 2–0 edge going into the seventh inning. Astros pitcher Zack Greinke had

allowed just one hit all night. The Houston crowd could sense a
championship coming.

Then Rendon strode to the plate. The third baseman had
been Washington's best player all season. And when the
Nats needed a big hit, he delivered. On a 1–0 count, Rendon
hammered a changeup to left field. Just like that, the lead was
cut in half.

After Kendrick's legendary two-run bomb in the seventh,
Washington reliever Patrick Corbin went back to work. He had
allowed no runs in the sixth, and then he went back out and
tossed two more shutout innings. Meanwhile, the Nationals
added some insurance runs.

In the eighth, Soto flicked a single to right field to score
Adam Eaton. Then in the ninth, Eaton broke the game open
with a two-run single. Daniel Hudson came on to pitch the
ninth and close out the Astros.

Hudson got Houston's George Springer to pop out. He then
struck out Jose Altuve swinging. Then, with the Astros down to
their last strike, he got Michael Brantley swinging on a slider.
Hudson heaved his glove in celebration as his teammates
rushed onto the field. Loyal Washington fans in attendance
yelled, jumped up and down, and hugged, as Brantley left
the batter's box in defeat. After 50 years as a franchise, the
Nationals were finally World Series champions.

Nationals pitcher Daniel Hudson celebrates the team's first World Series win in 2019. They defeated the Houston Astros 6–2 in Game 7.

Nationals slugger Juan Soto led all of baseball in on-base percentage in both the 2020 and 2021 seasons.

RELOADING

The Nationals could not maintain their World Series success. Before 2020 Rendon signed with the Los Angeles Angels. Washington slipped back to fifth place in the NL East.

Other stars left soon after. When Washington struggled to start the 2021 season, management decided it could not afford to keep Turner and Scherzer. Both players were traded to the Dodgers. Without them, the Nationals tumbled to a 65–97 record. It was time to rebuild.

Washington thought it had the perfect player to build around in Soto. General manager Mike Rizzo offered the young star a record 15-year, $440-million contract in the summer of 2022. But the 23-year-old outfielder turned it down. Instead, the Nationals dealt Soto and first baseman Josh Bell to the San Diego Padres at that year's trade deadline for several prospects.

There was still one familiar face left, as Strasburg was under contract for a few more years. Nationals fans might have to wait a little while for more World Series glory. But fresh memories of their first triumph would help them remember that victory is worth the wait.

TIMELINE

1968

Montreal is awarded one of two new National League teams to begin play the next season.

1969

The Montreal Expos take the field as the first MLB team in Canada.

1977

The Expos move into Olympic Stadium, their permanent home for the rest of their time in Montreal.

1979

The Expos have their first winning season but finish in second place.

1981

After winning the second half of a season interrupted by a players' strike, the Expos make the playoffs for the first time and beat the Philadelphia Phillies in the NLDS. A game-winning home run by the Los Angeles Dodgers' Rick Monday in the NLCS ends the Expos' run. Expos fans have named the day in their team's history "Blue Monday."

1991

Ace Dennis Martinez throws the first perfect game in Expos history.

1994

The Expos own the best record in baseball when a players' strike cancels the rest of the regular season and playoffs.

1995

Expos management begins a "fire sale" to get rid of the team's top players rather than award them new contracts.

2001

After the team is nearly eliminated, MLB steps in to take control of the Expos.

2003

The Expos play part of their home schedule in San Juan, Puerto Rico. The Expos return to Puerto Rico in 2004.

2004

On the day of the Expos' final home game of the season, MLB announces the team will be moving to Washington, DC, the following season.

2005

The newly renamed Washington Nationals play the first MLB game in the nation's capital since 1971.

2010

College star pitcher Stephen Strasburg makes his highly anticipated MLB debut with the Nationals.

2012

With teenage sensation Bryce Harper, the Nationals make the playoffs for the first time in Washington.

2019

After a slow start to the year, the Nationals rally with a run all the way to the World Series, where they win in a thrilling seven-game series.

TEAM FACTS

FRANCHISE HISTORY

Montreal Expos (1969–2004)
Washington Nationals (2005–)

WORLD SERIES CHAMPIONSHIPS

2019

KEY PLAYERS

Gary Carter (1974–84, 1992)
Andre Dawson (1976–86)
Vladimir Guerrero (1996–2003)
Bryce Harper (2012–18)
Pedro Martinez (1994–97)
Tim Raines (1979–90, 2001)
Max Scherzer (2015–21)
Juan Soto (2018–)
Rusty Staub (1969–71, 1979)
Stephen Strasburg (2010–)
Ryan Zimmerman
  (2005–19, 2021)

KEY MANAGERS

Felipe Alou (1992–2001)
Dave Martinez (2018–)
Frank Robinson (2002–06)

HOME STADIUMS

Jarry Park (1969–76)
Olympic Stadium (1977–2004)
Hiram Bithorn Stadium
  (2003–04)
RFK Stadium (2005–07)
Nationals Park (2008–)

MASCOT LEFT BEHIND

One uniformed member of the Expos did not make the move with the team to Washington. Mascot Youppi! instead became the mascot of the National Hockey League's Montreal Canadiens.

MR. EXPO

Felipe Alou managed the most games in Expos history. He was an employee of the team from 1976 to 2001, starting out as a coach before becoming manager in 1992.

RAISE THE ROOF

Montreal's Olympic Stadium was designed to have one of the first retractable roofs in sports. But the roof rarely worked properly and was opened and closed only 88 times. It was locked into place in 1992.

PRESIDENTIAL HISTORY

When President George W. Bush threw out the first pitch at RFK Stadium on April 4, 2005, it was exactly 95 years since William Taft began the presidential first pitch tradition at a game of the original Washington Nationals.

THE RACING PRESIDENTS

In addition to the ballgame, Nationals games have another heated competition, the Presidents Race. Racers wearing costumes of George Washington, Thomas Jefferson, Abraham Lincoln, and Teddy Roosevelt hold a footrace in the middle of the fourth inning to see who's the fastest.

GLOSSARY

ace

A team's best starting pitcher.

bullpen

The area on a baseball field where relief pitchers can warm up.

changeup

A pitch that looks like a fastball but is thrown much more slowly to deceive the hitter.

commissioner

The chief executive of a sports league.

journeyman

A player who has played for many teams or has been unable to find a specific role.

minor league

A lower level of baseball where players work on improving their skills before they reach the major leagues.

no-hitter

A complete game in which a team does not allow any hits.

perfect game

A complete game in which a team retires every opposing batter and allows no base runners.

players' strike

The players refuse to work due to a disagreement between them and their employers (teams) about things such as working conditions or wages.

shutout

A complete game in which a pitcher allows no runs.

slider

A pitch that often breaks down and away from the batter.

walk-off

Any victory in which the home team scores the winning run on its final plate appearance of the game.

MORE INFORMATION

BOOKS

Flynn, Brendan. *The MLB Encyclopedia*. Minneapolis, MN: Abdo Publishing, 2022.

Gitlin, Marty. *MLB*. Minneapolis, MN: Abdo Publishing, 2021.

Smith, Elliott. *Bryce Harper*. Minneapolis, MN: Abdo Publishing, 2018.

ONLINE RESOURCES

To learn more about the Washington Nationals, please visit **abdobooklinks.com** or scan this QR code. These links are routinely monitored and updated to provide the most current information available.

ABOUT THE AUTHOR

Anthony K. Hewson is a freelance writer who specializes in writing nonfiction for kids..